Property of:

____

Content:

Self Love

- Question Nr.1 -

Am I worthy of good things like love and happiness?

- Question Nr. 2 -

How do I show love for myself?

- Question Nr. 3 -

Do I speak up when I feel I'm not getting what I deserve?

- Question Nr. 4 -

How comfortable am I with saying "no" to things or people who do not bring me joy?

- Question Nr. 5 -

Do I feel guilty if I put my needs first?

- Question Nr. 6 -

When was the last time I felt beautiful?
Smart? Powerful?

- Question Nr. 7 -

If someone tells me I'm not good enough, how would I respond?

- Question Nr. 8 -

If someone tells me I'm amazing, how would I respond?

- Question Nr. 9 -

How often do I apologize, even when it's not my fault?

- Question Nr. 10 -

How often do I take on other people's problems as if they were my own?

- Question Nr. 11 -

When was the last time I told myself "good job"?

- Question Nr. 12 -

How often do I spend time and energy taking care of myself versus taking care of others?

Happiness

- Question Nr. 13 -

What are the top 5 things that bring a smile to my face?

- Question Nr. 14 -

How do I define the meaning of "joy"?

- Question Nr. 15 -

How important is my own happiness?

- Question Nr. 16 -

When was the last time I laughed so hard my belly ached?

- Question Nr. 17 -

How often do I have a positive experience versus a negative experience?

- Question Nr. 18 -

How content am I with life in general?

- Question Nr. 19 -

How would I answer the question
"I'll be happy when…"?

- Question Nr. 20 -

What's preventing me from being truly happy now?

- Question Nr. 21 -

What am I doing to increase my happiness?

- Question Nr. 22 -

Do I have any regrets that I can't let go?

- Question Nr. 23 -

When was the last time I let myself have a good cry?

- Question Nr. 24 -

What does a "happy life" look like in my mind?

- Question Nr. 25 -

How do I bring happiness to other people's lives?

- Question Nr. 26 -

Would my friends describe me as a "positive person"?

- Question Nr. 27 -

When was the last time I found the "silver lining" in a bad situation?

- Question Nr. 28 -

How do I express gratitude?

- Question Nr. 29 -

If I were to describe 3 things I'm grateful for right now, what would they be?

- Question Nr. 30 -

Do I believe I'm responsible for my own happiness?
Why or why not?

Resilience and Mindset

- Question Nr. 31 -

How do I respond to a tough challenge that really tests my limit?

- Question Nr. 32 -

How long does it usually take for me to bounce back from failure?

- Question Nr. 33 -

True or false: It takes a lot to knock me down.

- Question Nr. 34 -

What am I more afraid of?
Failure, or the regret of not trying?

- Question Nr. 35 -

How adaptable am I to changing circumstances and environments?

- Question Nr. 36 -

How often do I tell myself "I can't"?

- Question Nr. 37 -

When was the last time I encountered a frustrating situation and what did I do to make it better?

- Question Nr. 38 -

Do I believe I have control over how I feel and the experiences I have in life?

- Question Nr. 39 -

When was the last time I felt really disappointed or hurt? What helped me overcome it?

- Question Nr. 40 -

How often do I complain?

- Question Nr. 41 -

When was the last time I solved a tough problem and what did I learn from it?

Purpose and Motivation

- Question Nr. 42 -

What are some of the things that really demotivate me?

- Question Nr. 43 -

What helped me regain my motivation in the past when I lost it?

- Question Nr. 44 -

What excites me enough to keep me focused for hours on end?

- Question Nr. 45 -

What fuels me more: reward or fear of punishment?

- Question Nr. 46 -

What do I hope to achieve in life?

- Question Nr. 47 -

What am I doing on a day to day basis to progress towards my ultimate goal in life?

- Question Nr. 48 -

Do I think I'm doing something of value with my life? Why or why not?

- Question Nr. 49 -

In what ways am I contributing to the world?

- Question Nr. 50 -

What activities make me feel productive, engaged, and deeply content?

- Question Nr. 51 -

If money wasn't an issue, would I still be in my current job? If not, what would I like to do instead?

- Question Nr. 52 -

When was the last time I gave up on a goal?
Why did I give up?

- Question Nr. 53 -

Have I ever accomplished a goal only to find out it wasn't fulfilling for me? What kind of goal was it?

- Question Nr. 54 -

When was the last time I accomplished goal that made me feel good for long time? What kind of goal was it?

- Question Nr. 55 -

How do I go about making difficult decisions in life?

Personal Growth

- Question Nr. 56 -

When was the last time I did something that made me feel a little scared or uncomfortable?

- Question Nr. 57 -

What lessons did I learn from the last major mistake I made in my work?

- Question Nr. 58 -

What's my career goal for the next 5-10 years and how does it align with my ultimate goal in life?

- Question Nr. 59 -

What am I doing on a daily/weekly/monthly/yearly basis to improve myself?

- Question Nr. 60 -

Do I enjoy learning? If so, what am I doing to ensure that I keep learning?

- Question Nr. 61 -

In what ways have I grown as a person in the last year?

- Question Nr. 62 -

How comfortable am I with having a difficult, but necessary conversation with someone?

- Question Nr. 63 -

What traits of a good leader do I exhibit?

- Question Nr. 64 -

What traits of leadership do I need to work on?

- Question Nr. 65 -

What am I doing in the next 6-12 months to progress in my career?

Love

- Question Nr. 66 -

What are the 3 most important things I look for in a relationship in my current stage in life?

- Question Nr. 67 -

What do I think will be the 3 most important things I look for in a relationship 10 years from now?

- Question Nr. 68 -

What am I doing to improve the quality of my relationship?

- Question Nr. 69 -

Do I value being in a committed, loving relationship?
If so, how do I show it?

- Question Nr. 70 -

Am I willing to make compromises in a relationship?
If so, what kind of compromises?

- Question Nr. 71 -

How do I maintain my independence and sense of "self" in a relationship?

- Question Nr. 72 -

When I picture the kind of life I want to live with my partner, what does that look like?

- Question Nr. 73 -

How important is marriage for me, and why?

- Question Nr. 74 -

How would I respond if a partner hurt me deeply but is showing remorse?

- Question Nr. 75 -

What are the "dealbreakers" in a relationship for me?

- Question Nr. 76 -

What impact did my parents' relationship have on my view of relationship and marriage?

- Question Nr. 77 -

What skills do I think I need in order to have a successful relationship?

- Question Nr. 78 -

What qualities do I value the most in a partner, and why are they important?

- Question Nr. 79 -

What are the top 3 lessons I learned from my past relationships?

- Question Nr. 80 -

What's my primary love language?

- Question Nr. 81 -

How well do I communicate my needs in a relationship?

- Question Nr. 82 -

What's my fighting style and how does that impact my relationship?

Family

- Question Nr. 83 -

How important is family to me and how do I show it?

- Question Nr. 84 -

Why do I want (or don't want) to have children?

- Question Nr. 85 -

What's my way of showing love for my family?

- Question Nr. 86 -

Does my way of showing love align with how my family would like me to show love for them?

- Question Nr. 87 -

How satisfied am I with the relationships that I have with members of my family?

- Question Nr. 88 -

How do I go about resolving conflicts between myself and family members? How effective is my approach?

- Question Nr. 89 -

How do I show support for family members even if I don't agree with them?

- Question Nr. 90 -

How do I feel about being a stay-at-home parent?

- Question Nr. 91 -

Do I get enough appreciation from my family?

- Question Nr. 92 -

How comfortable am I talking to my family about my feelings?

Friendship

- Question Nr. 93 -

Do I have these qualities of a good friend and in what ways do I exhibit these traits?

- Question Nr. 94 -

Why are friendships important to me and how do I show it?

- Question Nr. 95 -

What do I prefer: socializing with a large group of friends or talk one on one?

- Question Nr. 96 -

Do I bring positivity into my friendships? If so, how?

- Question Nr. 97 -

What are the 3 most important qualities
I look for in a friend?

- Question Nr. 98 -

Do I have any unfulfilling friendships that are draining my energy and happiness?

- Question Nr. 99 -

What are my boundaries in a friendship?

- Question Nr. 100 -

How much time do I spend talking versus listening in my friendships?

- Question Nr. 101 -

How do I show appreciation for my friends?

- Question Nr. 102 -

How accepting am I of my friends' opinions and beliefs?

- Question Nr. 103 -

What does "having a good time with friends" look like for me?

Health

- Question Nr. 104 -

How important is my health to me and why?

- Question Nr. 105 -

What's the biggest obstacle standing between me and a health goal?

- Question Nr. 106 -

What does my diet look like and how does it make me feel?

- Question Nr. 107 -

How do I take care of my body?

- Question Nr. 108 -

How much control do I believe I have over my own health?

- Question Nr. 109 -

What am I doing to reduce and prevent stress?

- Question Nr. 110 -

How much sleep am I getting every night and what am I doing to improve the quality of my sleep?

- Question Nr. 111 -

Am I getting enough exercise despite my busy schedule?

- Question Nr. 112 -

What are 3 healthy habits I like to develop in the next 12 months?

Who You Are

- Question Nr. 113 -

If I was a Marvel superhero, who would I be and why?

- Question Nr. 114 -

Who's my celebrity crush and what do
I admire about them?

- Question Nr. 115 -

What words do I use the most often and how do they reflect me as a person?

- Question Nr. 116 -

What's one secret I wouldn't tell anybody and why?

- Question Nr. 117 -

What was my favorite TV show growing up and what impact did it have on me?

- Question Nr. 118 -

Who am I most jealous of and why?

- Question Nr. 119 -

What compliment do I like to hear the most?

- Question Nr. 120 -

If the apocalypse fell upon the world tomorrow, how long do I think I'd last?

Thank you!

We hope you enjoyed our book.

As a small family company, your feedback is very important to us .

Please let us know how you like our book at :

pickme.readme@gmail.com